ALICE'S ADVENTURES IN WONDERLAND

'We're all mad here, you know,' said the Cheshire Cat. 'I'm mad. You're mad.'

'How do you know that I'm mad?' said Alice.

'Of course you're mad,' said the Cheshire Cat. 'Only mad people come here.'

This is the story of Alice's dream, one hot summer day long ago. A dream of Wonderland, where the White Rabbit wears gloves and the Caterpillar smokes a pipe . . . where the Mad Hatter is always having tea with the March Hare, and where the Queen of Hearts wants to cut off everyone's head . . .

It's all very strange, but then, anything can happen in a dream world.

T0050540

OXFORD BOOKWORMS LIBRARY
Classics

Alice's Adventures in Wonderland

Stage 2 (700 headwords)

Series Editor: Jennifer Bassett
Founder Editor: Tricia Hedge
Activities Editors: Jennifer Bassett and Alison Baxter

LEWIS CARROLL

Alice's Adventures in Wonderland

Retold by
Jennifer Bassett

Illustrated by
Nilesh Mistry

OXFORD UNIVERSITY PRESS

OXFORD
UNIVERSITY PRESS

Great Clarendon Street, Oxford OX2 6DP

Oxford University Press is a department of the University of Oxford.
It furthers the University's objective of excellence in research, scholarship,
and education by publishing worldwide in

Oxford New York

Auckland Cape Town Dar es Salaam Hong Kong Karachi
Kuala Lumpur Madrid Melbourne Mexico City Nairobi
New Delhi Shanghai Taipei Toronto

With offices in

Argentina Austria Brazil Chile Czech Republic France Greece
Guatemala Hungary Italy Japan Poland Portugal Singapore
South Korea Switzerland Thailand Turkey Ukraine Vietnam

OXFORD and OXFORD ENGLISH are registered trade marks of
Oxford University Press in the UK and in certain other countries

ISBN 978 0 19 479051 2

A complete recording of this Bookworms edition of
Alice's Adventures in Wonderland is available.

Printed in China

Original illustration on p 50 by John Tenniel,
courtesy of Mary Evans Picture Library Ltd

Word count (main text): 6315 words

For more information on the Oxford Bookworms Library,
visit www.oup.com/elt/gradedreaders

CONTENTS

1
Down the rabbit-hole

*A*lice was beginning to get very bored. She and her sister were sitting under the trees. Her sister was reading, but Alice had nothing to do. Once or twice she looked into her sister's book, but it had no pictures or conversations in it.

'And what is the use of a book,' thought Alice, 'without pictures or conversations?'

She tried to think of something to do, but it was a hot day and she felt very sleepy and stupid. She was still sitting and thinking when suddenly a White Rabbit with pink eyes ran past her.

Suddenly a White Rabbit ran past her.

There was nothing really strange about seeing a rabbit. And Alice was not *very* surprised when the Rabbit said, 'Oh dear! Oh dear! I shall be late!' (Perhaps it *was* a little strange, Alice thought later, but at the time she was not surprised.)

But then the Rabbit *took a watch out of its pocket*, looked at it, and hurried on. At once Alice jumped to her feet.

'I've never before seen a rabbit with either a pocket, or a watch to take out of it,' she thought. And she ran quickly across the field after the Rabbit. She did not stop to think, and when the Rabbit ran down a large rabbit-hole, Alice followed it immediately.

After a little way the rabbit-hole suddenly went down, deep into the ground. Alice could not stop herself falling, and down she went, too.

It was a very strange hole. Alice was falling very slowly, and she had time to think and to look around her. She could see nothing below her because it was so dark. But when she looked at the sides of the hole, she could see cupboards and books and pictures on the walls. She had time to take things out of a cupboard, look at them, and then put them back in a cupboard lower down.

'Well!' thought Alice. 'After a fall like this, I can fall anywhere! I can fall downstairs at home, and I won't cry

Alice was falling very slowly.

or say a word about it!'

Down, down, down. 'How far have I fallen now?' Alice said aloud to herself. 'Perhaps I'm near the centre of the earth. Let me think . . . That's four thousand miles down.' (Alice was very good at her school lessons and could remember a lot of things like this.)

Down, down, down. Would she ever stop falling? Alice was very nearly asleep when, suddenly, she was sitting on the ground. Quickly, she jumped to her feet and looked around. She could see the White Rabbit, who was hurrying away and still talking to himself. 'Oh my ears and whiskers!' he was saying. 'How late it's getting!'

Alice ran after him like the wind. She was getting very near him when he suddenly turned a corner. Alice ran

3

round the corner too, and then stopped. She was now in a long, dark room with doors all round the walls, and she could not see the White Rabbit anywhere.

She tried to open the doors, but they were all locked. 'How will I ever get out again?' she thought sadly. Then she saw a little glass table with three legs, and on the top of it was a very small gold key. Alice quickly took the key and tried it in all the doors, but oh dear! Either the locks were too big, or the key was too small, but she could not open any of the doors.

Then she saw another door, a door that was only forty centimetres high. The little gold key unlocked this door easily, but of course Alice could not get through it – she was much too big. So she lay on the floor and looked through the open door, into a beautiful garden with green trees and bright flowers.

Alice looked through the door into a beautiful garden.

4

Poor Alice was very unhappy. 'What a wonderful garden!' she said to herself. 'I'd like to be out there – not in this dark room. Why can't I get smaller?' It was already a very strange day, and Alice was beginning to think that anything was possible.

After a while she locked the door again, got up and went back to the glass table. She put the key down and then she saw a little bottle on the table ('I'm sure it wasn't here before,' said Alice). Round the neck of the bottle was a piece of paper with the words DRINK ME in large letters.

But Alice was a careful girl. 'It can be dangerous to drink out of strange bottles,' she said. 'What will it do to me?' She drank a little bit very slowly. The taste was very nice, like chocolate and oranges and hot sweet coffee, and very soon Alice finished the bottle.

* * *

'What a strange feeling!' said Alice. 'I think I'm getting smaller and smaller every second.'

And she was. A few minutes later she was only twenty-five centimetres high. 'And now,' she said happily, 'I can get through the little door into that beautiful garden.'

She ran at once to the door. When she got there, she remembered that the little gold key was back on the glass table. She ran back to the table for it, but of course, she was now much too small! There was the key, high above her, on top of the table. She tried very hard to climb up the table leg, but she could not do it.

At last, tired and unhappy, Alice sat down on the floor and cried. But after a while she spoke to herself angrily.

'Come now,' she said. 'Stop crying at once. What's the use of crying?' She was a strange child, and often talked to herself like this.

Soon she saw a little glass box near her on the floor. She opened it, and found a very small cake with the words EAT ME on it.

Nothing could surprise Alice now. 'Well, I'll eat it,' she said. 'If I get taller, I can take the key off the table. And if I get smaller, I can get under the door. One way

Alice tried very hard to climb up the table leg.

6

or another, I'll get into the garden. So it doesn't matter what happens!'

She ate a bit of the cake, and then put her hand on top of her head. 'Which way? Which way?' she asked herself, a little afraid. Nothing happened. This was not really surprising. People don't usually get taller or shorter when they

In the glass box there was a very small cake.

eat cake. But a lot of strange things were happening to Alice today. 'It will be very boring,' she said, 'if *nothing* happens.'

So she went on eating, and very soon the cake was finished.

2
The pool of tears

'*C*uriouser and curiouser!' said Alice. (She was very surprised, and for a minute she forgot how to speak good English.)

'I shall be as tall as a house in a minute,' she said. She

tried to look down at her feet, and could only just see them. 'Goodbye, feet!' she called. 'Who will put on your shoes now? Oh dear! What nonsense I'm talking!'

Just then her head hit the ceiling of the room. She was now about three metres high. Quickly, she took the little gold key from the table and hurried to the garden door.

Poor Alice! She lay on the floor and looked into the garden with one eye. She could not even put her head through the door.

She began to cry again, and went on crying and crying. The tears ran down her face, and soon there was a large pool of water all around her on the floor. Suddenly she heard a voice, and she stopped crying to listen.

'Oh, the Duchess, the Duchess! She'll be so angry! I'm late, and she's waiting for me. Oh dear, oh dear!'

It was the White Rabbit again. He was hurrying down the long room, with some white gloves in one hand and a large fan in the other hand.

Alice was afraid, but she needed help. She spoke in a quiet voice. 'Oh, please, sir—'

The Rabbit jumped wildly, dropped the gloves and the fan, and hurried away as fast as he could.

Alice picked up the fan and the gloves. The room was very hot, so she began to fan herself while she talked. 'Oh dear! How strange everything is today! Did I change in the night? Am I a different person today? But if I'm a

The Rabbit jumped wildly, and dropped the gloves and the fan.

different person, then the next question is – *who* am I? Ah, that's the mystery.'

She began to feel very unhappy again, but then she looked down at her hand. She was wearing one of the Rabbit's white gloves. 'How did I get it on my hand?' she thought. 'Oh, I'm getting smaller again!' She looked round the room. 'I'm already less than a metre high. And getting smaller every second! How can I stop it?' She saw the fan in her other hand, and quickly dropped it.

She was now very, very small – and the little garden door was locked again, and the little gold key was lying on the glass table.

'Things are worse than ever,' thought poor Alice. She turned away from the door, and fell into salt water, right up to her neck. At first she thought it was the sea, but then she saw it was the pool of tears. Her tears. Crying makes a lot of tears when you are three metres tall.

'Oh, why did I cry so much?' said Alice. She swam around and looked for a way out, but the pool was very big. Just then she saw an animal in the water near her. It looked like a large animal to Alice, but it was only a mouse.

'Shall I speak to it?' thought Alice. 'Everything's very strange down here, so perhaps a mouse can talk.'

So she began: 'Oh Mouse, do you know the way out of this pool? I am very tired of swimming, oh Mouse!' (Alice did not know if this was the right way to speak to a mouse. But she wanted to be polite.)

The mouse looked at her with its little eyes, but it said nothing.

'Perhaps it doesn't understand English,' thought Alice. 'Perhaps it's a French mouse.' So she began again,

It looked like a large animal to Alice, but it was only a mouse.

and said in French: 'Where is my cat?' (This was the first sentence in her French lesson-book.)

The mouse jumped half out of the water and looked at her angrily.

'Oh, I'm so sorry!' cried Alice quickly. 'Of course, you don't like cats, do you?'

'Like cats?' cried the mouse in a high, angry voice. 'Does any mouse like cats?'

'Well, perhaps not,' Alice began kindly.

But the mouse was now swimming quickly away, and soon Alice was alone again. At last she found her way out of the pool and sat down on the ground. She felt very lonely and unhappy. But after a while the White Rabbit came past again, looking for his white gloves and his fan.

'The Duchess! The Duchess! Oh my ears and whiskers! She'll cut my head off, I know she will! Oh, where *did* I drop my gloves?' Then he saw Alice. 'Why, Mary Ann, what are you doing here? Run home at once, and bring me some gloves and a fan. Quick, now!'

Alice hurried away. 'But where is his house?' she thought while she ran. Strangely, she was no longer in the long room with the little door, but outside in a wood. She ran and ran but could not see a house anywhere, so she sat down under a flower to rest.

3
Conversation with a caterpillar

'Now,' Alice said to herself. 'First, I must get a little bigger, and second, I must find my way into that beautiful garden. I think that will be the best plan. But oh dear! *How* shall I get bigger? Perhaps I must eat or drink something, but the question is, what?'

Alice looked all around her at the flowers and the trees, but she could not see anything to eat. Then she saw a large mushroom near her. It was as tall as she was. She walked across to look at it, and there, on top of the mushroom, was a large caterpillar, smoking a pipe. After a while, the Caterpillar took the pipe out of its mouth and said to Alice in a slow, sleepy voice, 'Who are *you*?'

'I don't really know, sir,' said Alice. 'I know who I *was* when I got up this morning, but I have changed so often since then. I think I am a different person now.'

'What do you mean by that?' said the Caterpillar. 'Explain yourself!'

'I can't explain *myself*, sir,' said Alice, 'because I'm not myself, you know.'

'I don't know,' said the Caterpillar.

'Explain yourself!' said the Caterpillar.

'It's difficult to describe,' Alice replied politely. 'One minute I'm very small, the next minute I'm as tall as a house, then I'm small again. Usually, I stay the same all day, and changing so often feels very strange to me.'

'You!' said the Caterpillar, in a very unfriendly voice. 'Who are *you?*'

They were now back at the beginning of their conversation, which was not very helpful. Alice felt a little cross and decided to walk away.

'Come back!' the Caterpillar called after her. 'I've something important to say.'

This sounded better, so Alice turned back.

'Never get angry,' said the Caterpillar.

'Is that all?' said Alice, trying not to be angry.

'No,' said the Caterpillar. For some minutes it smoked its pipe and did not speak, but at last it took the pipe out of its mouth, and said, 'So you've changed, have you? How tall do you want to be?'

'I would like to be a *little* larger, sir, please,' said Alice. 'Eight centimetres is really very small.'

For a while the Caterpillar smoked its pipe. Then it shook itself, got down off the mushroom, and moved slowly away into the grass. It did not look back at Alice, but said, 'One side will make you taller, and the other side will make you shorter.'

'One side of *what?*' thought Alice to herself.

She did not say this aloud, but the Caterpillar said, 'Of the mushroom.' Then it moved away into the wood.

Alice looked at the mushroom carefully, but it was round, and did not have sides. At last she broke off a piece in each hand from opposite sides of the mushroom.

She ate some of the piece in her left hand, and waited to see what would happen.

A minute later her head was as high as the tallest tree in the wood, and she was looking at a sea of green leaves. Then a bird appeared and began to fly around her head, screaming, 'Egg thief! Egg thief! Go away!'

'I'm *not* an egg thief,' said Alice.

'Oh no?' said the bird angrily. 'But you eat eggs, don't you?'

'Well, yes, I do, but I don't *steal* them,'

'Egg thief! Egg thief! Go away!' screamed the bird.

15

explained Alice quickly. 'We have them for breakfast, you know.'

'Then how do you get them, if you don't steal them?' screamed the bird.

This was a difficult question to answer, so Alice brought up her right hand through the leaves and ate a little from the other piece of mushroom. She began to get smaller at once and, very carefully, she ate first from one hand, then from the other, until she was about twenty-five centimetres high.

'That's better,' she said to herself. 'And now I must find that garden.' She began to walk through the wood, and after a while she came to a little house.

4

The Cheshire Cat

There was a boy outside the door, with a large letter in his hand. (He was dressed like a boy, but his face was very like a fish, Alice thought.) The Fish-Boy knocked at the door, and a second later a large plate came flying out of an open window.

'A letter for the Duchess,' the Fish-Boy shouted. He pushed the letter under the door and went away.

Alice went up to the door and knocked, but there

'A letter for the Duchess,' the Fish-Boy shouted.

was a lot of noise inside and nobody answered. So she opened the door and walked in.

She found herself in a kitchen, which was full of smoke. There was a very angry cook by the fire, and in the middle of the room sat the Duchess, holding a screaming baby. Every few minutes a plate crashed to the floor. There was also a large cat, which was sitting on a chair and grinning from ear to ear.

'Please,' Alice said politely to the Duchess, 'why does your cat grin like that?'

'It's a Cheshire Cat,' said the Duchess. 'That's why.'

'I didn't know that cats *could* grin,' said Alice.

'Well, you don't know much,' said the Duchess. Another plate crashed to the floor and Alice jumped. 'Here!' the Duchess went on. 'You can hold the baby for a bit, if you like. The Queen has invited me to play

There was a large cat, which was grinning from ear to ear.

croquet, and I must go and get ready.' She pushed the baby into Alice's arms and hurried out of the room.

'Oh, the poor little thing!' said Alice, looking at the baby, which had a very strange face. She took it outside into the wood and walked around under the trees. Then the baby began to make strange noises, and Alice looked into its face again. Its eyes were really very small for a baby, and its nose now looked very like the nose of a pig.

'Don't make noises like that, my dear,' said Alice. 'It's not polite. You're beginning to sound like a pig.'

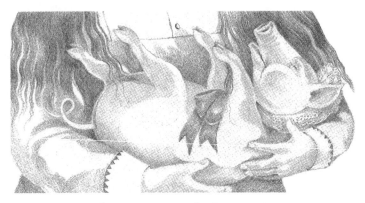

There was no mistake. It was a pig.

But a few minutes later, there was no mistake. It *was* a pig. Alice put it carefully on the ground, and it ran quietly away on its four legs into the wood.

'I'm pleased about that,' Alice said to herself. 'It will be a good-looking pig, but it would be terrible to be a child with a face like that.'

She was thinking about pigs and children when she suddenly saw the Cheshire Cat in a tree. The Cat grinned at her, and she went nearer to it.

'Please,' she said, 'can you tell me which way to go from here?'

'But where do you want to get to?' said the Cat.

'It doesn't really matter—' began Alice.

'Then it doesn't matter which way you go,' said the Cat.

'But I would like to get *somewhere*,' Alice explained.

'If you just go on walking,' said the Cat, 'in the end you'll arrive somewhere.'

That was true, thought Alice, but not very helpful, so she tried another question. 'What kind of people live near here?'

'To the left,' the Cat said, 'lives a Hatter. And to the right, lives a March Hare. You can visit either of them. They're both mad.'

'But I don't want to visit mad people,' said Alice.

'We're all mad here, you know,' said the Cat. 'I'm mad. You're mad.'

'How do you know that I'm mad?' said Alice.

'Of course you're mad,' said the Cat. 'Only mad people come here.'

Alice was thinking about this, but the Cat went on, 'Are you playing croquet with the Queen today?'

'I would like to very much,' said Alice, 'but nobody has invited me yet.'

'You'll see me there,' said the Cat, and vanished.

Alice was not really surprised at this, because so many strange things were happening today. She was still looking at the tree when, suddenly, the Cat appeared again.

'I forgot to ask,' said the Cat. 'What happened to the baby?'

'It turned into a pig,' Alice said.

'I'm not surprised,' said the Cat, and vanished again.

Alice began to walk on, and decided to visit the March Hare. 'It's the month of May now,' she said to herself, 'so perhaps the Hare won't be as mad as he was in March.'

Suddenly, there was the Cheshire Cat again, sitting in another tree. Alice jumped in surprise.

'Do you think,' she said politely, 'that you could come and go more slowly?'

'All right,' said the Cat. And this time it vanished very slowly. First its tail went, then its body, then its head, and last, the grin.

'Well! I've often seen a cat without a grin,' thought Alice, 'but never a grin without a cat!'

Soon she saw the house of the March Hare in front of her. It was a large house, so she ate a little piece of mushroom to get bigger, and walked on.

This time the cat vanished very slowly.

5
A mad tea-party

There was a table under a tree outside the house, and the March Hare and the Hatter were having tea. A Dormouse was sitting between them, asleep. The three of them were all sitting together at one corner of the table, but the table was large and there were many other seats. Alice sat down in a big chair at one end.

'Have some coffee,' the March Hare said in a friendly voice.

Alice looked all round the table, but she could only see a teapot. 'I don't see any coffee,' she said.

'There isn't any,' said the March Hare.

'Then why did you ask me to have some?' said Alice crossly. 'It wasn't very polite of you.'

'It wasn't very polite of you to sit down. We haven't invited you to tea,' said the March Hare.

'But there are lots of seats,' said Alice.

'Your hair's too long,' said the Hatter, looking at Alice with interest.

'It's not polite to say things like that,' said Alice.

The Hatter looked surprised, but he said, 'Why is a bird like a desk?'

Alice was pleased. She enjoyed playing wordgames, so she said, 'That's an easy question.'

The March Hare and the Hatter were having tea.

'Do you mean you know the answer?' said the March Hare.

'Yes,' said Alice.

'Then you must say what you mean,' the March Hare said.

'I do,' Alice said quickly. 'Well, I mean what I say. And that's the same thing, you know.'

'No, it isn't!' said the Hatter. 'Listen to this. *I see what I eat* means one thing, but *I eat what I see* means something very different.'

Alice did not know what to say to this. So she took some tea and some bread-and-butter while she thought about it. The Dormouse woke up for a minute and then went to sleep again. After a while the Hatter took out his watch, shook it, then looked at it sadly.

'Two days slow! I told you that butter wasn't good for watches!' he said angrily to the March Hare.

'It was the *best* butter,' said the March Hare sadly.

Alice was looking at the watch with interest. 'It's a strange watch,' she said. 'It shows the day of the week, but not the time.'

'But we know the time,' said the Hatter. 'It's always six o'clock here.'

Alice suddenly understood. 'Is that why there are all these cups and plates?' she said. 'It's always tea-time here, and you go on moving round the table. Is that right? But what happens when you come to the beginning again?'

'Don't ask questions,' said the March Hare crossly. 'You must tell us a story now.'

'But I don't know any stories,' said Alice.

Then the March Hare and the Hatter turned to the Dormouse. 'Wake up, Dormouse!' they shouted loudly in its ears. 'Tell us a story.'

'Yes, please do,' said Alice.

The Dormouse woke up and quickly began to tell a story, but a few minutes later it was asleep again. The March Hare poured a little hot tea on its nose, and the Hatter began to look for a clean plate. Alice decided to leave and walked away into the wood. She looked back once, and the March Hare and the Hatter were trying to put the Dormouse into the teapot.

The March Hare poured a little hot tea
on the Dormouse's nose.

'Well, I won't go *there* again,' said Alice. 'What a stupid tea-party it was!' Just then she saw a door in one of the trees. 'How curious!' she thought. 'But everything is strange today. I think I'll go in.'

So she went in. And there she was, back in the long room with the little glass table. At once, she picked up the gold key from the table, unlocked the little door into the garden, and then began to eat a piece of mushroom. When she was down to about thirty centimetres high, she walked through the door, and then, at last, she was *in* the beautiful garden with its green trees and bright flowers.

6
The Queen's game of croquet

*N*ear the door there was a rose-tree and three gardeners, who were looking at the roses in a very worried way.

'What's the matter?' Alice said to them.

'You see, Miss,' said the first gardener, 'these roses are white, but the Queen only likes *red* roses, and she—'

'The Queen!' said the second gardener suddenly, and at once, the three gardeners lay down flat on their faces. Alice turned round and saw a great crowd of people.

It was a pack of cards, walking through the garden. There were clubs (they were soldiers), and diamonds, and ten little children (they were hearts). Next came some Kings and Queens. Then Alice saw the White Rabbit, and behind him, the Knave of Hearts. And last of all, came *THE KING AND QUEEN OF HEARTS*.

When the crowd came near to Alice, they all stopped and looked at her, and the Queen said, 'Who are you?'

'My name is Alice, Your Majesty,' said Alice very politely. But she thought to herself, 'They're only a pack of cards. I don't need to be afraid of them!'

'And who are *these*?' said the Queen, looking at the three gardeners. Then she saw the white roses, and her

It was a pack of cards, walking through the garden.

face turned red and angry. 'Off with their heads!' she shouted, and soldiers hurried up to take the gardeners away. The Queen turned to Alice. 'Can you play croquet?' she shouted.

'Yes!' shouted Alice.

'Come on, then!' shouted the Queen. The crowd began to move on, and Alice went with them.

'It's – it's a very fine day,' said a worried voice in her ear. Alice saw that the White Rabbit was by her side.

'Very fine,' said Alice. 'Where's the Duchess?'

'Shhh!' said the Rabbit in a hurried voice. 'She's in prison, waiting for execution.'

'What for?' said Alice.

But just then the Queen shouted, 'Get to your places!' and the game began.

It was the strangest game of croquet in Alice's life! The balls were hedgehogs, and the mallets were flamingoes. And the hoops were made by soldiers, who turned over and stood on their hands and feet. Alice held her flamingo's body under her arm, but the flamingo turned its long neck first this way and then that way. At last, Alice was ready to hit the ball with the flamingo's head. But by then, the hedgehog was tired of waiting and was walking away across the croquet-ground. And when both the flamingo and the hedgehog were ready, there was no hoop! The soldiers too were always getting up and walking away. It really was a very difficult game, Alice thought.

The players all played at the same time, and they were always arguing and fighting for hedgehogs. Nobody could agree about anything. Very soon, the Queen was wildly angry, and went around shouting 'Off with his head!' or 'Off with her head!' about once a minute.

Alice began to feel worried. 'The Queen is sure to argue with me soon,' she thought. 'And what will happen to me then? They're cutting people's heads off all the time here. I'm surprised there is anyone left alive!'

Just then she saw something very strange. She watched carefully, and after a minute or two she saw that the

The balls were hedgehogs, and the mallets were flamingoes.

thing was a grin. 'It's the Cheshire Cat,' she said to herself. 'Now I'll have somebody to talk to.'

'How are you getting on?' said the Cat, when its mouth appeared.

Alice waited. 'I can't talk to something without ears,' she thought. Slowly the Cat's eyes, then its ears, and then the rest of its head appeared. But it stopped at the neck, and its body did not appear.

Alice began to tell the Cat all about the game. 'It's very difficult to play,' she said. 'Everybody argues all the time, and the hoops and the hedgehogs walk away.'

'How do you like the Queen?' said the Cat quietly.

'I don't,' said Alice. 'She's very—' Just then she saw the Queen behind her, so she went on, '—clever. She's the best player here.'

The Queen smiled and walked past.

'Who *are* you talking to?' said the King. He came up behind Alice and looked at the Cat's head in surprise.

'It's a friend of mine – a Cheshire Cat,' said Alice.

'I'm not sure that I like it,' said the King. 'But it can touch my hand if it likes.'

'I prefer not to,' said the Cat.

'Well!' said the King angrily. He called out to the Queen, 'My dear! There's a cat here, and I don't like it.'

The Queen did not look round. 'Off with its head!' she shouted. 'Call for the executioner!'

Alice was a little worried for her friend, but when the executioner arrived, everybody began to argue.

'I can't cut off a head,' said the executioner, 'if there isn't a body to cut it off from.'

'You can cut the head off,' said the King, 'from anything that's got a head.'

'If somebody doesn't do something quickly,' said the Queen, 'I'll cut everybody's head off.'

Nobody liked that plan very much, so they all turned to Alice. 'And what do *you* say?' they cried.

'*Off with its head!*' *the Queen shouted.*

'The Cat belongs to the Duchess,' said Alice carefully. 'Perhaps you could ask *her* about it.'

'She's in prison,' the Queen said to the executioner. 'Bring her here at once.'

But then the Cat's head slowly began to vanish, and when the executioner came back with the Duchess, there was nothing there. The King ran wildly up and down, looking for the Cat, and the Duchess put her arm round Alice. 'I'm so pleased to see you again, my dear! ' she said.

'Let's get on with the game,' the Queen said angrily, and Alice followed her back to the croquet-ground.

The game went on, but all the time the Queen was arguing, and shouting 'Off with his head!' or 'Off with her head!' Soon there were no hoops left, because the soldiers (who were the hoops) were too busy taking everybody to prison. And at the end there were only three players left – the King, the Queen, and Alice.

The Queen stopped shouting and said to Alice, 'Have you seen the Mock Turtle yet?'

'No,' said Alice. 'I'm not sure what a Mock Turtle is.'

'Then come with me,' said the Queen.

They found the Mock Turtle down by the sea. Next to him was a Gryphon, asleep in the sun. Then the Queen hurried away, saying, 'I have to get on with some executions.'

The Gryphon woke up, and said sleepily to Alice, 'It's just talk, you know. They never execute anybody.'

Alice was pleased to hear this. She felt a little afraid of the Gryphon and the Mock Turtle, because they were so large. But they were very friendly, and sang songs and told her many stories about their lives. The Mock Turtle

The Mock Turtle and the Gryphon were very friendly.

34

was in the middle of a very sad song when they all heard a shout a long way away: 'It's beginning!'

'Come on! We must hurry!' cried the Gryphon. It took Alice by the hand and began to run.

7
Who stole the tarts?

*T*he King and Queen of Hearts were sitting on their thrones when Alice and the Gryphon arrived. There was a great crowd of birds and animals, and all the pack of cards.

Soldiers stood all around the Knave of Hearts, and near the King was the White Rabbit, with a trumpet in one hand.

In the middle of the room there was a table, with a large plate of tarts on it. 'They look good,' thought Alice, who was feeling a little hungry.

Then the White Rabbit called out loudly, 'Silence! The trial of the Knave of Hearts will now begin!' He took out a long piece of paper, and read:

> *The Queen of Hearts, she made some tarts,*
> *All on a summer day.*
> *The Knave of Hearts, he stole those tarts,*
> *And took them all away.*

On the table was a large plate of tarts.

'Very good,' said the King. 'Call the first witness.'

Alice looked at the jury, who were now writing everything down. It was a very strange jury. Some of the jurymen were animals, and the others were birds.

Then the White Rabbit blew his trumpet three times, and called out, 'First witness!'

The first witness was the Hatter. He came in with a

teacup in one hand and a piece of bread-and-butter in the other hand. 'I'm very sorry, Your Majesty,' he said. 'I was in the middle of tea when the trial began.'

'Take off your hat,' the King said.

'It isn't mine,' said the Hatter.

'*Stolen!* Write that down,' the King said to the jury.

'I keep hats to sell,' explained the Hatter. 'I don't have a hat myself. I'm a Hatter.'

'Give your evidence,' said the King, 'or we'll cut your head off.'

The Hatter's face turned white. 'I'm a poor man, Your Majesty,' he began, in a shaking voice.

Just then Alice had a strange feeling. After a minute or two she understood what it was.

'Don't push like that,' said the Dormouse, who was sitting next to her. 'I'm nearly falling off my seat.'

'I'm very sorry,' Alice said politely. 'I'm getting bigger and taller, you see.'

'Well, you can't do that *here*,' said the Dormouse crossly, and he got up and moved to another seat.

The Hatter was still giving evidence, but nobody could understand a word of it. The King looked at the Queen, and the Queen looked at the executioner.

The unhappy Hatter saw this, and dropped his bread-and-butter. 'I'm a poor man, Your Majesty,' he said again.

The unhappy Hatter dropped his bread-and-butter.

'You're a *very* poor *speaker*,' said the King. He turned to the White Rabbit. 'Call the next witness,' he said.

The next witness was the Duchess's cook, who spoke very angrily and said that she would not give any evidence. The King looked worried and told the White Rabbit to call another witness. Alice watched while the White Rabbit looked at the names on his piece of paper. Then, to her great surprise, he called out loudly, 'Alice!'

'Here!' cried Alice, jumping to her feet.

'What do you know about these tarts?' said the King.

'Nothing,' said Alice.

The Queen was looking hard at Alice. Now she said, 'All people a mile high must leave the room.'

'I'm not a mile high,' said Alice. 'And I won't leave the room. I want to hear the evidence.'

'There is no more evidence,' said the King very quickly, 'and now the jury will—'

'Your Majesty!' said the White Rabbit, jumping up in a great hurry. 'We've just found this letter. There's no name on it, but I think the Knave wrote it.'

'No, I didn't!' said the Knave loudly.

'Read it to us,' said the King.

'Where shall I begin, Your Majesty?' asked the Rabbit.

'Begin at the beginning,' said the King, 'and go on until you get to the end, then stop.'

Everybody listened very carefully while the White Rabbit read these words.

> *They tell me you have been to her,*
> *And talked of me to him.*
> *She thought I was a gardener,*
> *But said I could not swim.*
>
> *He tells them that I have not gone,*
> *(We know that this is true).*
> *If she decides to hurry on,*
> *What will they do to you?*
>
> *I gave her one, they gave him two,*
> *You gave us three or more.*
> *They all returned from him to you,*
> *But they were mine before.*

'That's a very important piece of evidence,' said the King. He looked very pleased. 'Now the jury must—'

'If anybody in the jury can explain that letter,' said Alice (she was not afraid of anything now, because she was much bigger than everybody in the room), 'I'll give him sixpence. It's all nonsense! It doesn't mean anything.'

The jury busily wrote this down. '*She* thinks it's all nonsense.'

'All nonsense, eh?' said the King. He read some of the words again. '*But said I could not swim.* You can't swim, can you?' he said to the Knave.

The Knave's face was sad. 'Do I look like a swimmer?' he said. (And he didn't – because he was made of paper.)

The King smiled. 'I understand everything now,' he said. 'There are the tarts, and here is the Knave of Hearts. And now the jury must decide who the thief is.'

'No, no!' said the Queen. 'Off with his head! The jury can say what it thinks later.'

'What nonsense!' said Alice loudly. 'The jury must decide *first*. You can't—'

'Be quiet!' said the Queen, her face turning red.

'I won't!' said Alice.

'Off with her head!' screamed the Queen. Nobody moved.

'It doesn't matter what you say,' said Alice. 'You're only a pack of cards!'

Then the pack of cards flew up into the sky and began to fall on Alice's face. She gave a little scream . . .

Then the pack of cards began to fall on Alice's face.

and woke up. She was lying next to her sister under the trees, and some leaves were falling on her face.

'Wake up, Alice dear,' said her sister. 'You've been asleep a long time.'

'Oh, I've had a *very* curious dream!' said Alice, and she told her sister all about the strange adventures in her wonderful dream.

GLOSSARY

appear to come where somebody can see you

argue to talk angrily with someone when you do not agree

croquet a game using mallets to knock balls through small hoops

curious strange ('good English' – see page 7 – would be *more curious*, not *curiouser*)

dream a picture in your head when you are asleep

duchess the title of an important woman

evidence information about something or someone given at a law trial

execution cutting somebody's head off

grin a big, friendly smile

invite to ask someone to come somewhere, or to do something

jury twelve people at a trial who listen to the evidence and then decide if someone is a criminal or not

mad ill in the head

nonsense silly or stupid talk or ideas

polite saying things like 'please' and 'thank you' is polite

sadly unhappily

trial the time when people (a judge, a jury, etc.) decide if someone has done something wrong

vanish to go away very quickly or surprisingly

witness somebody who gives evidence at a trial

worried feeling that something is wrong

Your Majesty words that you say when talking to a queen or king

Alice's Adventures in Wonderland

ACTIVITIES

Before Reading

1 Read the back cover and the story introduction on the first page. Who does Alice meet in Wonderland? Tick the right boxes for the answers.

Alice meets . . .

☐ a policeman ☐ a rabbit ☐ a hare ☐ her sister
☐ a chicken ☐ a horse ☐ a cat ☐ a queen
☐ a caterpillar ☐ a king ☐ a dog ☐ a hatter

2 What does Alice do in the story? Tick the right boxes.

Alice . . .

☐ goes to a tea-party   ☐ wears gloves
☐ plays tennis   ☐ talks to a cat
☐ smokes a pipe   ☐ plays croquet
☐ falls down a rabbit-hole   ☐ cuts off someone's head

3 Who will say these words in the story? Can you guess?

1 'Oh, where *did* I drop my gloves?'
2 'I told you that butter wasn't good for watches!'
3 'You can visit either of them. They're both mad.'
4 'Off with his head!'
5 'How strange everything is today!'

While Reading

Read Chapter 1, and put these sentences in the right order.

1 Alice found a small key and unlocked a very small door.
2 Alice fell down a rabbit-hole.
3 Alice drank something from a bottle and got very small.
4 Alice ate a small cake, which said, 'EAT ME'.
5 Alice saw a White Rabbit and ran after him.
6 Alice tried to climb up a table leg to get the key again.

Before you read Chapter 2, can you guess what will happen? Choose one ending for this sentence.

When Alice has finished eating the cake, she will . . .
a) be ill.   b) get smaller.   c) get bigger.   d) wake up.

Read Chapter 2. Here are some untrue sentences about it. Change them into true sentences.

1 Alice was soon as small as a mouse.
2 The Duchess dropped her gloves and fan.
3 The fan made Alice get bigger.
4 Alice fell into the sea.
5 While she was swimming, Alice met a cat.
6 Alice suddenly found herself outside in a garden.

Read Chapter 3. Choose the best question-word for these questions, and then answer them.

What / Why

1 . . . did the Caterpillar tell Alice to do?
2 . . . couldn't Alice explain herself?
3 . . . did the Caterpillar call Alice back?
4 . . . did Alice have to eat if she wanted to get bigger?
5 . . . did the bird call Alice?
6 . . . didn't Alice answer the question about stealing eggs?

Read Chapters 4 and 5. Choose the best words to complete this summary of the chapters.

When Alice went into the Duchess's *kitchen / bedroom*, there was a cat which was *screaming / grinning*, and a baby who was *screaming / grinning*. The Duchess *gave / took* the baby *from / to* Alice, but the baby *was / turned into* a pig. After that Alice *had / spoke* a conversation with the Cheshire Cat and they talked *to / about* mad people.

At the tea-party the March Hare said, 'Have some *coffee / tea*,' but there wasn't *some / any*. Later, he said to Alice, 'You must *mean / say* what you *mean / say*.' The Hatter had a watch which *showed / didn't show* the time because it was *always / never* six o'clock there. The tea-party *always / never* finished, and they just went on *moving / moved* round the table. Alice thought it was a very *clever / stupid* tea-party and went away.

Before you read Chapter 6 (*The Queen's game of croquet*), can you guess what happens?
Tick one box each time.

	YES	NO
1 Alice wins the game of croquet.	☐	☐
2 The Queen wants to cut lots of heads off.	☐	☐
3 Alice meets some more strange animals.	☐	☐
4 When the game finishes, Alice wakes up.	☐	☐

Read Chapters 6 and 7. Match these halves of sentences.

1 The croquet game was very strange . . .

2 The Queen of Hearts got very angry . . .

3 Then Alice saw her friend the Cheshire Cat, . . .

4 The King didn't like the Cat's head . . .

5 But the executioner couldn't cut off a head . . .

6 After the croquet there was a jury trial to find out . . .

7 While the Hatter was giving his evidence, . . .

8 At the end Alice began to argue with the Queen, . . .

9 but only its head appeared, not its body.

10 and then she woke up.

11 because everybody had to use flamingoes for mallets.

12 who stole the tarts made by the Queen of Hearts.

13 and wanted to cut it off.

14 Alice was getting bigger and taller.

15 and sent nearly everybody to prison.

16 if there wasn't a body to cut it off from.

After Reading

1 Here is Alice, telling her sister about her dream. But it is difficult to remember dreams, and Alice gets a lot of things wrong. Can you find her mistakes and correct them?

ALICE: Well, first I saw a brown rabbit, who took a clock out of his bag, and then I fell down a mouse-hole.

SISTER: Oh dear! Were you afraid?

ALICE: Oh no. I fell very quickly, you see. And when I ate or drank things, I got fatter or thinner. I talked to a caterpillar who was sitting under a mushroom, and I also talked to a Duchess. Oh yes, and there was a baby that turned into a fish. Then I played croquet – but for balls we had flamingoes, and the mallets were hedgehogs.

SISTER: There were a lot of animals in your dream.

ALICE: Yes, there were. There was also a Cheshire Cat who cried, and I had lunch with a March Hare and a Hatter—

SISTER: A hatter?

ALICE: Yes, you know, a man who buys hats. He was one of the jurymen who gave evidence at the trial—

SISTER: What trial was that?

ALICE: Oh, somebody ate some tarts. But the evidence was all nonsense, and the King of Hearts wanted to cut people's heads off all the time.

SISTER: Cut their heads off? That's terrible!

ALICE: They didn't really cut people's heads off, you know. They were just a box of cards – made of wood.

2 **Later, Alice wrote a song about her dream. Fill in the gaps with seven of these words. For each gap, there are two possible words. Which are they, and why is one of them better? (Think about the *sound* of the word.)**

around, away, building, change, Clubs, Hearts, here, him, house, me, mean, show, there, turn

One day I had a curious dream,

But now I ask, 'What did it _____?'

I saw a cat up in a tree,

Who spoke as well as you or _____.

In a pool of tears I met a mouse,

And then a Hatter outside a _____,

Having tea with a mad March Hare.

Perhaps they're both still sitting _____.

And then there was a plate of tarts,

Made by the angry Queen of _____.

Her croquet game was hard to play;

The hoops and balls just walked _____.

The jury trial was also strange,

But then the cards began to _____

into leaves

and I woke up.

3 Here is an illustration for the story by a famous artist, John Tenniel. Find the best place in the story to put the picture, and answer these questions.

The picture goes on page _____.

1 Who are the characters in this picture?

2 What are two of them doing?

3 Where is Alice at this moment?

Now write a caption for the illustration.

Caption: _____

4 Can you find the 19 words hidden in this word search? Words go from left to right, or from top to bottom.

R	R	A	B	B	I	T	H	P	L	A	T	E	P
P	M	O	U	S	E	C	E	M	H	A	R	E	L
M	B	C	A	K	E	A	D	B	X	C	B	G	A
A	U	B	A	L	L	T	G	F	O	C	R	H	Y
L	T	A	Q	T	D	R	E	A	M	U	E	O	E
L	T	L	I	A	P	W	H	E	D	P	A	O	R
E	E	Y	Z	R	I	E	O	H	F	T	D	P	E
T	R	T	S	T	G	F	G	T	E	A	P	O	T
O	J	E	C	A	T	E	R	P	I	L	L	A	R

Now put the words from the word search into groups under these three headings. There is one word which does not belong to any of the groups. What is it?

CROQUET	TEA-TIME	ANIMALS

5 Write a short passage about *your* dreams. Use some of these notes to help you.

- my dreams / full of / exciting adventures / frightening things / strange things / don't understand them
- sometimes / always / never / dream about / family / friends / strangers / animals
- sometimes in a dream / can / can't / fly / move
- always / never / dream about / same / different things
- wake up in the night / remember / next day / forget

51

ABOUT THE AUTHOR

Lewis Carroll (his real name was Charles Lutwidge Dodgson) was born in 1832, and was the third child of a family of eleven children. When he was a child, Charles was very good at writing word games and puzzles, and later he was also good at Latin and mathematics. He went to Rugby School, and then to Christ Church at the University of Oxford. He taught mathematics at Christ Church from 1855 until his death in 1898.

Dodgson wrote books about mathematics, and he was also a very good photographer, but his most famous work is *Alice's Adventures in Wonderland*. It began as a story told to a real little girl, called Alice Liddell, during a boat trip on the river one summer, and was published as a book in 1865. A second story about Alice, called *Through the Looking-Glass and What Alice Found There*, followed in 1871, and in 1876 came his third famous nonsense book, *The Hunting of the Snark*. The two *Alice* stories, full of clever word games and verses, are among the most famous children's books ever written. They were also important because they were the first stories for children which did not try to teach them how to be good.

Alice's Adventures in Wonderland is read by both adults and children; it has been translated into many languages, made into plays for the theatre, and filmed many times. The characters in Alice's dream are now part of our language – we talk of people 'grinning like a Cheshire cat', or being 'as mad as a hatter'. And when anything strange happens, we often say, just like Alice in her dream, 'Curiouser and curiouser'.

OXFORD BOOKWORMS LIBRARY

Classics • Crime & Mystery • Factfiles • Fantasy & Horror
Human Interest • Playscripts • Thriller & Adventure
True Stories • World Stories

The OXFORD BOOKWORMS LIBRARY provides enjoyable reading in English, with a wide range of classic and modern fiction, non-fiction, and plays. It includes original and adapted texts in seven carefully graded language stages, which take learners from beginner to advanced level. An overview is given on the next pages.

All Stage 1 titles are available as audio recordings, as well as over eighty other titles from Starter to Stage 6. All Starters and many titles at Stages 1 to 4 are specially recommended for younger learners. Every Bookworm is illustrated, and Starters and Factfiles have full-colour illustrations.

The OXFORD BOOKWORMS LIBRARY also offers extensive support. Each book contains an introduction to the story, notes about the author, a glossary, and activities. Additional resources include tests and worksheets, and answers for these and for the activities in the books. There is advice on running a class library, using audio recordings, and the many ways of using Oxford Bookworms in reading programmes. Resource materials are available on the website <www.oup.com/elt/gradedreaders>.

The *Oxford Bookworms Collection* is a series for advanced learners. It consists of volumes of short stories by well-known authors, both classic and modern. Texts are not abridged or adapted in any way, but carefully selected to be accessible to the advanced student.

You can find details and a full list of titles in the *Oxford Bookworms Library Catalogue* and *Oxford English Language Teaching Catalogues*, and on the website <www.oup.com/elt/gradedreaders>.

THE OXFORD BOOKWORMS LIBRARY
GRADING AND SAMPLE EXTRACTS

STARTER • 250 HEADWORDS

present simple – present continuous – imperative –
can/cannot, must – *going to* (future) – simple gerunds …

Her phone is ringing – but where is it?

Sally gets out of bed and looks in her bag. No phone. She looks under the bed. No phone. Then she looks behind the door. There is her phone. Sally picks up her phone and answers it. *Sally's Phone*

STAGE I • 400 HEADWORDS

… past simple – coordination with *and, but, or* –
subordination with *before, after, when, because, so* …

I knew him in Persia. He was a famous builder and I worked with him there. For a time I was his friend, but not for long. When he came to Paris, I came after him – I wanted to watch him. He was a very clever, very dangerous man. *The Phantom of the Opera*

STAGE 2 • 700 HEADWORDS

… present perfect – *will* (future) – *(don't) have to, must not, could* –
comparison of adjectives – simple *if* clauses – past continuous –
tag questions – *ask/tell* + infinitive …

While I was writing these words in my diary, I decided what to do. I must try to escape. I shall try to get down the wall outside. The window is high above the ground, but I have to try. I shall take some of the gold with me – if I escape, perhaps it will be helpful later. *Dracula*

STAGE 3 • 1000 HEADWORDS

... should, may – present perfect continuous – *used to* – past perfect –
causative – relative clauses – indirect statements ...

Of course, it was most important that no one should see
Colin, Mary, or Dickon entering the secret garden. So Colin
gave orders to the gardeners that they must all keep away
from that part of the garden in future. *The Secret Garden*

STAGE 4 • 1400 HEADWORDS

... past perfect continuous – passive (simple forms) –
would conditional clauses – indirect questions –
relatives with *where/when* – gerunds after prepositions/phrases ...

I was glad. Now Hyde could not show his face to the world
again. If he did, every honest man in London would be
proud to report him to the police. *Dr Jekyll and Mr Hyde*

STAGE 5 • 1800 HEADWORDS

... future continuous – future perfect –
passive (modals, continuous forms) –
would have conditional clauses – modals + perfect infinitive ...

If he had spoken Estella's name, I would have hit him. I was
so angry with him, and so depressed about my future, that I
could not eat the breakfast. Instead I went straight to the old
house. *Great Expectations*

STAGE 6 • 2500 HEADWORDS

... passive (infinitives, gerunds) – advanced modal meanings –
clauses of concession, condition

When I stepped up to the piano, I was confident. It was as if I
knew that the prodigy side of me really did exist. And when
I started to play, I was so caught up in how lovely I looked
that I didn't worry how I would sound. *The Joy Luck Club*

BOOKWORMS • CLASSICS • STAGE 2

The Jungle Book

RUDYARD KIPLING

Retold by Ralph Mowat

In the jungle of Southern India the Seeonee Wolf-Pack has a new cub. He is not a wolf – he is Mowgli, a human child, but he knows nothing of the world of men. He lives and hunts with his brothers the wolves. Baloo the bear and Bagheera the panther are his friends and teachers. And Shere Khan, the man-eating tiger, is his enemy.

Kipling's famous story of Mowgli's adventures in the jungle has been loved by young and old for more than a hundred years.

BOOKWORMS • FANTASY & HORROR • STAGE 2

Five Children and It

EDITH NESBIT

Retold by Diane Mowat

When the children dug a hole in the gravel-pit, they were very surprised at what they found. 'It' was a Psammead, a sand-fairy, thousands of years old.

It was a strange little thing – fat and furry, and with eyes on long stalks. It was often very cross and unfriendly, but it could give wishes – one wish a day. 'How wonderful!' the children said.

But wishes are difficult things. They can get you into trouble . . .